THE
TRUTH
MATTERS

BRUCE
BARTLETT

THE
TRUTH
MATTERS

A CITIZEN'S GUIDE
TO SEPARATING FACTS
FROM LIES AND STOPPING
FAKE NEWS IN ITS TRACKS

10
TEN SPEED PRESS
California | New York

Published in the United States by Ten Speed Press, an imprint of the
Crown Publishing Group, a division of Penguin Random House LLC,
New York.
www.crownpublishing.com
www.tenspeed.com

Ten Speed Press and the Ten Speed Press colophon are registered
trademarks of Penguin Random House LLC.

Library of Congress Cataloging-in-Publication Data
Names: Bartlett, Bruce R., 1951- author.
Title: The truth matters : a citizen's guide to separating facts from lies
    and stopping fake news in its tracks / Bruce Bartlett.
Description: First edition. | California, N.Y. : Ten Speed Press, 2017. |
    Includes bibliographical references and index.
Identifiers: LCCN 2017028338 (print) | LCCN 2017029755 (ebook) |
Subjects: LCSH: Journalism—History—21st century. | Attribution of news. |
    News audiences.
Classification: LCC PN4815.2 (ebook) | LCC PN4815.2 .B37 2017 (print) |
    DDC 070.90/51—dc23
LC record available at https://lccn.loc.gov/2017028338

Hardcover ISBN: 978-0-399-58116-8
eBook ISBN: 978-0-399-58117-5

Printed in the United States of America

Design by Emma Campion

10 9 8 7 6 5 4 3 2 1

First Edition

To all the journalists who gave
their lives to bring us the news.

———————

CONTENTS

INTRODUCTION

Once upon a time, Americans could read their local newspaper, subscribe to a weekly newsmagazine, and watch thirty minutes of national news on television each night, and be reasonably sure they knew everything important and newsworthy that they needed to know to live their lives.

Those days are long gone. Newspapers have shrunk their news coverage drastically, the newsweeklies are shadows of their former selves, and the network evening broadcasts are viewed by only a fraction of their previous viewership.

At the same time, there are now a number of cable news channels that broadcast twenty-four hours a day, every day; virtually every traditional news source is now available on the Internet; and there are thousands of new Internet news sources constantly competing for our attention.

News junkies love the proliferation of news outlets and the many new ways of obtaining it—on their phones, on Twitter, Facebook, and elsewhere. But the average person is overwhelmed by the cacophony of information. Many simply tune out altogether and have become less informed about the news that affects them, while others consume only the sliver of news that interests them, whether it be sports, entertainment, or the stock market. When it comes to politics, there is a growing tendency to obtain news only from sources favorable to one's ideological or partisan point of view.

Many people crave a simpler time before cable and the Internet, but of course it is impossible to put the toothpaste back in the tube. Rather, we must adapt to the evolving news landscape. We must also learn to be more discerning about our news sources and beware of "fake news" or "alternative facts," which are propagated by people interested only in maximizing clicks, even if it means peddling lies and half-truths, or even by foreign governments using our own freedom of speech against us to pursue their own agenda at our expense.

Like it or not, people will have to acquire their own news, to a certain extent, and must therefore learn journalistic techniques and various tricks of the trade. Fortunately, the Internet makes this relatively easy. The methods I outline in this book are those I have used myself for decades that have served me well in my roles as staff director of a congressional committee, member of the White House staff, and syndicated columnist. I have often been amazed to discover that reporters at top newspapers such as the *New York Times* have been unaware of them, perhaps because many are still wedded to journalism school methods learned in the pre-Internet era.

My model is a famous book, *The Elements of Style,* by William Strunk Jr. and E. B. White. Generations of writers have learned how to write from this simple book, much of which consists of grammatical rules we all learned at one time but forgot or didn't entirely understand. I expect that much of what I write in this book will be equally familiar in terms of news gathering and consumption, but I also expect every reader, from savvy citizens to professional journalists, to come away with some tips they were unaware of. Many of the resources I mention throughout are assembled in the Suggested Resources appendix.

1

WHY THE TRADITIONAL MEDIA NO LONGER SERVES OUR NEEDS

KEY POINTS:

- The fairness doctrine is obsolete and cannot be revived.

- Conservatives were underserved for many years by traditional media.

- Progressives were slow to embrace new media such as talk radio.

People have never been happy with the news media, always blaming it for lying, misinforming, and being unfair to one side or the other. Thomas Jefferson expressed views on this subject that many people today no doubt would share. In an 1807 letter to John Norvell, Jefferson wrote,

> To your request of my opinion of the manner in which a newspaper should be conducted, so as to be most useful, I should answer, "by restraining it to true facts & sound principles only." Yet I fear such a paper would find few subscribers. It is a melancholy truth, that a suppression of the press could not more completely deprive the nation of its benefits, than is done by its abandoned prostitution to falsehood. Nothing can now be believed which is seen in a newspaper. Truth itself becomes suspicious by being put into that polluted vehicle. The real extent of this state of misinformation is known only to those who are in situations to confront facts within their knowledge with the lies of the day....
>
> I will add, that the man who never looks into a newspaper is better informed than he who reads

them; inasmuch as he who knows nothing is nearer to truth than he whose mind is filled with falsehoods & errors. He who reads nothing will still learn the great facts, and the details are all false.[1]

The complaint that the news media has a built-in bias is an old one—and there is truth in it. In Jefferson's day, newspapers were often owned by political parties and were very overt in their bias. Nowadays, the argument is that the major media has a liberal bias. The major media has long been based in cities, where people tend to be more socially liberal. Additionally, people with a liberal disposition have tended to gravitate to journalism as a profession.

Media consolidation also tended to make newspapers more liberal. In any town with more than one newspaper, one would usually be conservative, if only for competitive reasons. Partisan affiliation and ideological compatibility in editorials and news judgment and among columnists was one reason people subscribed

---

1   Thomas Jefferson, "From Thomas Jefferson to John Norvell, 11 June 1807," *National Archive*, Founders Online, founders.archives.gov/documents/Jefferson/99-01-02-5737.

to a particular paper. But as newspapers have closed, those with a conservative bent have tended to be the first to go, because they were usually the afternoon papers. Those with no competition tend toward bland mushiness when it comes to politics.

Radio and television news coverage always tended to be more evenhanded, because news presentation focused on breaking stories for which audio or video was available. It didn't lend itself to commentary or editorializing. Moreover, there was a government rule called the fairness doctrine that required both sides to be present when political endorsements were made or opinions expressed. But the main effect of this rule was to discourage the presentation of any opinions at all, rather than waste precious air time presenting alternative viewpoints.

In 1987, the fairness doctrine was abolished. Many rue this day as the one when fairness itself began to disappear from the media. But the fairness doctrine never applied to the print media, and it was already clear by 1987 that cable—CNN went on the air in 1980—was ushering in a new era of news coverage. It was untenable to maintain restrictions on over-the-air media

THE TRUTH MATTERS

that didn't apply to print publications or cable. It's likely that if the fairness doctrine hadn't been repealed, it would have been struck down by the courts.

It is indisputable, however, that abolition of the fairness doctrine gave rise to talk radio. Developments in the radio market were also critical; the AM band had been suffering for years, as the FM band was better suited to music. Rush Limbaugh was the first to recognize that the end of the fairness doctrine meant he could do an entire show devoted to nothing but expressing his opinions, of which he had many, all strongly felt and vigorously expressed. The AM band was well suited to talk, which was also cheaper than employing disc jockeys to curate music selections.

It's perhaps an accident of history that a strong conservative like Limbaugh was first to recognize the political potential of talk radio. It was probably also true that conservatives were underserved by the liberal sameness of conventional journalism at the time. At least in his early years, Limbaugh was a genuine news source, giving national attention to stories, research, and viewpoints that were hard to find elsewhere. Before his show, the only national outlets with a broad reach that reflected a conservative bent were the *Wall Street Journal* and *Reader's Digest*.

Limbaugh's success led to the creation of Fox News by Australian media mogul Rupert Murdoch, based on a vision long nurtured by Republican media guru Roger Ailes. With most television tilting a bit to the left, they cleverly positioned Fox in the middle of the political spectrum, which made it slightly to the right of its competitors.

The enormous financial success of conservative talk radio and Fox News stimulated growth of a vast conservative media network. Meanwhile, efforts by progressives to copy its success have uniformly failed. No one is quite sure why; it may be that those on the left are inclined to be satisfied with the traditional mainstream media. The problem is, mainstream media is dying a slow death. Something will replace it; we don't know yet just what that will be. Many analysts believe that virtually all news publications now in print will disappear in a few years.

It may be that progressives have more to gain from developing new methods of acquiring news and information than conservatives, who seem very satisfied with the availability of compatible news and views on Fox, talk radio, and the Internet. But conservatives should avoid complacency. With their closed loop of news sources, they are more prone to deception by charlatans peddling conspiracy theories, fake news, and extreme views far outside the mainstream. These are likely to be political albatrosses in the future.

In the long run, political parties and movements are best served by truth, accuracy, and responsible news reporting. It may be that this needs to be subsidized in some way. The federal government has long done this by giving newspapers and magazines subsidized mailing rates, and radio and television stations were given extremely valuable spectrum for literally nothing. Legal requirements that certain public notices be published in local newspapers are another sort of government subsidy. Given the importance of a well-informed electorate to the functioning of democracy, it is not unreasonable to think that market forces alone may be inadequate to the job.

One idea I have had is to allow foundations and other groups to endow reporting positions at news organizations, as has long been common for university professorships. Something like this is already being done at the *Boston Globe,* where local nonprofits are subsidizing the cost of employing a music critic, with the paper retaining full editorial control over the critic's work. If this practice were expanded, it could do much to support the kind of quality reporting that requires the backing of a salary to produce.

2

THE DIFFERENCE BETWEEN PRIMARY AND SECONDARY SOURCES

KEY POINTS:

- Primary sources are generally more reliable than secondary sources.

- The quality of evidence varies, and documentary sources are usually best.

- There are good reasons why officials leak information; not all are nefarious.

When reading or listening to any news report, we must evaluate the underlying source of the information to determine its truth or veracity. By underlying source, I don't necessarily mean the reporter or the news organization; rather, we must determine whether the reporting relies on someone with direct personal knowledge or the report is basically hearsay—something heard elsewhere by someone who cannot vouch for its truth.

If I personally witness an event, if I am present at a meeting where something occurred, if I am discussing something I personally did—these are all examples of primary sources. If I am repeating something someone told me, which is secondhand information, and the ultimate, original source is unidentified, this is a less reliable source.

This is not to say that all primary sources should be taken at face value; people lie, or they misremember, or they have some ax to grind that causes them to shade the truth in some way—by, for example, leaving out some critical piece of information in otherwise truthful statements.

This is why on crime shows like *CSI* the investigators always say that eyewitness accounts are often unreliable. It is better to rely on the forensic evidence gathered from the crime scene. So too with journalism. This is why documentary evidence is often preferred even to eyewitness accounts.

Examples of documentary evidence would include things like tax returns, because people can be punished by tax authorities for untruthful statements, or contracts, because lies can lead to litigation, or other sources of information where there is reason to believe that people have an incentive to be truthful.

Evaluating the veracity of either testimony or documentary evidence may depend on how close it is to the event in question. A statement or document produced shortly after an event occurs is likely to be more reliable than, say, a memoir produced many years later, although it may still be preferred to a secondary source. Thus one would probably place more weight on a diary entry or a memo written immediately after an important meeting than a published memoir that may be self-serving or based on selective memory.

Obviously, as a casual reader you cannot be expected to research every statement of fact you come across in the news or on social media. That is the job of the journalist. But you can keep an eye out for terminology that would lead you to either trust or be suspicious of some fact or evidence that is being used to justify a conclusion.

In the case of a reporter, was she actually there when some politician made a statement? If not, is there a reference or a link to the original source? These days it is very easy to embed audio or video online, and one can often listen or watch to see if a quote is accurate and whether the person is being quoted in proper context and is therefore a valid primary source, or is someone with an ax to grind who is passing on hearsay.

Politicians frequently assert greater knowledge than they actually have. Having worked on Capitol Hill for many years, at the Treasury Department and the White House, I know I often gave interviews based not on personal experience or inside knowledge but on what I had read in the paper that day. In a sense, it was a case of the blind leading the blind.

But not entirely. On any given day there could be competing facts or explanations for something the administration was doing. As an insider, I might know which was right or which was wrong. Simply by virtue of being in the milieu where policies were being discussed or personally knowing the people involved, I might be able to separate a likely true scenario from one that is probably false. This was of value to reporters, even if I got my basic information from the media in the first place.

When you're an insider, you need to always be vigilant when divulging some piece of information known to only a very limited number of people. This could allow a "leak" to be traced back to you and get you in trouble. In the vast majority of cases, leaks are harmless or even intentional. All you have done is deprive someone higher in the pecking order from releasing the information herself, thereby garnering chits with some reporter who may repay it with a "puff piece" later on.

It is also unfortunately true that reporters are much more likely to write about (and perhaps believe) something they think is a leak than an official announcement of the same information. There is actually a practical reason for this. An official announcement, such as a press release, is available to all reporters simultaneously and therefore of no special value to any one of them. Certain news organizations that strive to be comprehensive in their reporting, such as the Associated Press, may report it, but many others will ignore it as being inherently unnewsworthy.

On the other hand, if a reporter receives a leak, it is like having an exclusive. If she can get that information out quickly, she will scoop all her competitors. The problem is, some people who offer up leaks or exclusives may be lying. They may be gambling that a reporter is more interested in a scoop than in accuracy. The source may be sending up a trial balloon—putting forth a proposal before it has been agreed on, to test its popularity or viability. The columnists Robert Evans and Robert Novak were notorious for being willing to float trial balloons in return for a scoop.

Reputable reporters will not take leaks at face value. They will know that they may be being manipulated by their source. The reporter will seek out confirmation and will question the source to find out if she is a primary source with direct knowledge or just passing along hallway gossip. Unfortunately, deadline pressure makes such responsible journalism harder to do. There are always news outlets willing to publish first and ask questions later. Sadly, this has led to a race to the bottom, in which disreputable news outlets get the clicks and make the money, while those that are responsible and perform due diligence lose out.

Let me say a word about anonymous sources. Basically, everyone hates them, readers and reporters alike. But they are a necessary part of doing business where bosses want to tightly control the news and avoid releasing important information that the public has a right to know. Generally speaking, all "leaks" are anonymous; otherwise they would be official and on the record. But not all anonymous sources are leaks. Sometimes the information from an anonymous source is totally innocuous; it just didn't come from someone officially empowered to release it. Or a reporter may not want to divulge her source lest it point her competitors to it.

3

HOW TO USE LINKS

KEY POINTS:

- Links are like footnotes—essential documentation for facts.

- Writers need to be more discerning about their use of links, helping to guide readers.

- The quality of a source needs evaluation before including a link to it.

It has long been recognized that documentation is essential for an argument to have credibility and therefore persuasiveness. The traditional method of documentation is the footnote. Not surprisingly, lawyers have long been its greatest fan; it's not uncommon to read a law review article in which more than half of every page consists of footnotes with extremely detailed references.

Journalism has never embraced the footnote, but historically journalists have attempted to provide some degree of documentation in the text of an article. The problem is, they are often loath to credit a competitor for documentation. It's historically rare for a *Washington Post* story to give credit to the *New York Times* for breaking a story or vice versa, but not as rare as it used to be. A *Post* reporter may learn some important fact by reading the *Times,* but rather than repeat what the *Times* said, the *Post* reporter will call the same source and then pretend that this fact was independently acquired. There have been many occasions when I was the source of some story and was forced to repeat myself over and over again just so a publication didn't have to credit a competitor.

Another problem with journalistic documentation is that newspapers and magazines historically have been space-constrained. This often led them to be excessively vague about where certain information came from. A reporter may cite a "government study" without ever mentioning the author, the title, the agency that produced it, or the date it appeared. I have spent a considerable amount of time over the years tracking down such studies to see if they have been accurately portrayed or if they contained important qualifications or additional information. Often this proved impossible, even in the Internet age, which made me doubt the validity of a news report.

One of the great innovations of the Internet is the link, which theoretically solves the problem of documentation. A bit of text is highlighted, and by clicking it the reader is taken to a source that documents some fact or quotation. Unfortunately, links have not proven to be as useful as they should be.

One obvious problem is that links are useless in print publications; you have to be reading online to use them. Another is that even after all these years, some readers seem persistently unwilling to click them. Perhaps they have a slow computer connection or don't wish to be distracted. Whatever the reason, it constantly amazes me when people demand that I provide documentation for something I wrote, even though I provided a link that would have given them exactly what they wanted.

Many publishers have never embraced links, fearing that it will take readers away to other websites from which they may not return. Link rot—links that cease to work—is a constant problem. And of course there has long been a problem with pay walls and registration requirements. Although most pay-walled publications will allow free access to a limited number of articles each month, many readers resist registering to do so, perhaps fearful of getting a lot of spam in return. Note that full access can sometimes be obtained at no cost, as some papers will allow full access to anyone with a dot-edu email address. These are typically given to college students, but may be available to alumni as well.

The biggest problem I have with links is the lack of context when linking. The bit of text that is highlighted is not necessarily relevant to what the link documents. Until you actually click on the link and see where it takes you, you have no way of knowing its usefulness or even its relevance. In the old days, there was a footnote at the bottom of the page, so you could satisfy your curiosity with a quick glance. Even if you never checked a reference, often you could determine its credibility by seeing whether the source was a known expert in the subject, whether it was published in a reputable journal, and whether the source was contemporaneous.

A related problem is that writers are often very slipshod about the quality of the source to which they link. Frequently a link takes me to a secondary source of dubious quality when it would have taken little additional effort for the writer to find and provide a primary source for the point being linked. I know that sometimes this is done because the primary source may be unwieldy or excessively dense. Some people don't like to read PDF (portable document format) documents because they require special software and may take considerable time to download. Personally, I like PDF files because they are easier to print, and I find that the old-fashioned method of printing and filing documents is still the best way to save research.

It would help readers a great deal, I believe, if writers would take the time and effort to track down the best available source before linking and to think of links more as essential documentation than an FYI to the reader that simply clutters the text with extraneous material. In this respect, writers should say more in the text about the nature of their documentation. Instead of simply stating a fact and embedding a link, they could explain where the fact came from and say something about its nature. If it's a government study, don't just say "government study"; say, "According to a study published by the Bureau of Labor Statistics in the April 2017 issue of the *Monthly Labor Review* . . . ." The goal should be to give enough information that someone could find the source relatively easily even if the link didn't exist.

Because of link rot, I find it is often better to link to a home page whose address is unlikely to ever change and give readers a title that can be searched. Or I may suggest a couple of words that can be put into a search engine that will take them to the source I am referencing. As with footnotes, making the effort to provide additional information to the reader greatly improves a writer's credibility, makes it easier for readers to understand the basis for factual claims, and encourages people to use links as they were intended.

The potential for links is enormous in terms of helping to establish trust between a writer and the publication she writes for, on the one hand, and readers and news consumers, on the other. If people can see exactly where a fact came from and satisfy themselves that it is a primary source or a credible one, they are more likely to believe that fact even if it runs counter to what they would prefer to believe for partisan or other reasons.

I wish the media would create and use a new type of link, one that is more like a footnote, where a writer could embed the sort of information typically found in a footnote, such as the author, title, publication, location, and date of a source. People could satisfy their curiosity to some extent without having to click through but could do so if they want to, just as they do with links now. At present, hovering over a link just pops up the URL (universal resource locator), which is like a mailing address; it tells you very little—sometimes nothing—about the nature of a source without clicking through.

In short, both readers and writers need to learn the how and when of making better use of links. I consider them essential, as both a reader and a writer. But they could be much more useful if everyone better understood how to use them.

4

CONFUSING PRESS CONVENTIONS

KEY POINTS:

- The terms "on the record," "off the record," and "on background" have different meanings.

- These terms can be abused by sources to mislead reporters.

- Don't be afraid to use these conventions yourself when interacting with reporters.

One reason why news consumers have become dissatisfied with the mainstream media is that journalists follow many conventions that are seldom, if ever, spelled out to readers. Reporters, editors, and, sometimes, sources know them, but otherwise they remain a mystery.

One source of confusion is use of the term "off the record." Adding to the confusion, I have found over the years that different reporters and news organizations use this term differently, which can ensnare those inexperienced in dealing with the media and readers alike, creating confusion and embarrassment.

To start with, when a source reveals something "on the record," that simply means that whatever the source says may be quoted directly and that person may be named in the story along with other relevant information, such as their job title and some discussion of what ax they may have to grind. For example, an official spokesperson for a corporation or government agency is not at liberty to give their personal opinion on a matter; they are simply conveying an institutional point of view. Nevertheless, reporters will still try to get the spokesperson to say something contrary to the official view in hopes of getting a response that will spice up an otherwise ordinary story.

In my experience, speaking off the record means that a reporter can quote what a source says, but they may not be identified by name or title. They are generally identified by a vague descriptor such as "administration official" to show that they are in a position to know, but are not authorized to speak for the administration. As I mentioned in chapter 2, some people tend to equate all off-the-record statements with leaks, but they aren't necessarily the same thing. Often the person being quoted has simply decided to give an exclusive to one media source, for strategic reasons, and doesn't want to incur the ire of other news organizations.

However, I know that some news organizations use the term "off the record" more strictly. Back in 2004, Leonard Downie Jr., then executive editor of the *Washington Post,* said that in his paper's usage, "off-the-record information may not be used at all, either in the newspaper or in further reporting." He would consider my use of "off the record" to mean "not for attribution."

In my experience, Downie's definition of off the record is closer to the term "on background." To me, that term has always meant that a reporter can use the information I give her, but I cannot be quoted directly and my name may not be mentioned. I may also want an even more vague description of who I am to avoid getting in trouble with my bosses.

A related term is "deep background." In this instance, nothing you say to a reporter can be quoted, attributed, or written about at all unless it is confirmed by an unrelated source. Information derived from a deep background discussion is simply to guide a reporter's thinking or research.

Even long after I was out of government, I would still occasionally give interviews to reporters on background or deep background when I wanted to speak freely, without having to watch every word for fear of inadvertently misstating some fact or point in a way that would embarrass me or do harm to my ideological or political goals. Indeed, some reporters would call me and immediately tell me the discussion was on background to put me at ease because they were just

THE TRUTH MATTERS

trying to understand something that might or might not end up in a news story.

I sometimes would tell a reporter that they could quote me from a background interview, but that they needed to clear the quote with me in advance. I simply wanted to make sure I was accurately quoted on some point that might be highly technical or confusing. I have never found a reporter unwilling to abide by such a request, which aids both of us by ensuring accuracy while encouraging an open discussion.

Perhaps the master of using these various methods of giving interviews was Ronald Reagan's White House chief of staff James A. Baker. In that position, he often gave on-the-record interviews expressing the administration's position on the issues. But sometimes Baker disagreed with those positions, so he would simultaneously give the same reporter an off-the-record comment arguing against the position he had just expressed!

Despite my experience with the media, there have been times when I am caught off guard. Some years ago I wrote a column praising a book by the Pulitzer Prize–winning journalist Ron Suskind. He had sought me out from time to time and we would chat about various things the George W. Bush administration was doing. Since at the time he was not employed by any news organization, I viewed our conversations as between friends rather than reporter and source.

Then one day I got a call from a *New York Times Magazine* fact checker, saying that I was being quoted in an upcoming article by Suskind. The fact checker did not read my quotes to me or indicate their context, but simply asked whether I said this or that. I said that I did. I was often quoted in the *Times*, and I gave it no further thought.

A few days later, however, I learned that the Suskind article had been distributed to news organizations, and I was very extensively quoted making disparaging comments about President Bush. Although I was quoted accurately, it was embarrassing to me because I worked for a conservative think tank that was closely allied with the administration. Bush's top political adviser, Karl Rove, called my boss directly to complain that I was not being a team player, and I was berated for my comments. I was later fired by this organization after writing a book that was critical of Mr. Bush.

Ironically, my principal criticism was that Bush was not sufficiently committed to conservative principles, a view no conservative would disagree with today.

Thus one can see that it is not only those working in government who must be careful what they say to the media. Even those ostensibly free to speak must be careful lest their comments run afoul of some partisan, ideological, religious, or other line and subject them to criticism or even loss of a job.

Needless to say, this problem is very much more difficult in today's era of social media, which thankfully did not exist when I was in government. Today it is common for reporters to follow everything posted on social media by people who may in some way be newsworthy, and to mine past comments when someone is suddenly thrust into the media's attention. Employers often do the same; early in the Trump administration there were several instances where people had been hired for administration jobs, only to lose them when it was discovered that they had made disparaging comments about Mr. Trump on Twitter or Facebook or elsewhere. Oddly, though, some administration officials who worked for one of his competitors for the Republican presidential nomination—such as Kellyanne Conway, who worked for Senator Ted Cruz before switching to Trump—were forgiven for attacks they had made against Trump while serving in that capacity.

All this means that being careful about what one says in public is no longer just a problem for those working in government or even those who deal directly with the news media. Trying to keep everything you say private is one strategy, but it's difficult if you are trying to have a political impact by supporting a certain candidate or political action—such as the Women's March on Washington on January 21, 2017—or simply venting personal frustration over a governmental policy that isn't working. What's important is to express yourself deliberately, but carefully, whether you're on a public forum or in conversations or interviews.

5

JOURNALISTIC TECHNIQUES THAT MAY OBFUSCATE RATHER THAN ILLUMINATE SOURCES

KEY POINTS:

- Readers say they want only the facts, but in practice they demand context for stories.

- Editors and journalistic standards ensure truthfulness at reputable publications.

- Reputable publications correct their errors promptly and prominently.

M ost journalistic techniques were developed in an era when stories needed to be printed on paper to be seen and read. This was a very costly operation. Paper is expensive, and stories had to be set in type by highly skilled linotype machine operators; then the papers were distributed and sold by hand. Consequently, space was tight, and a reporter might have only a few column inches to tell her story, which meant using abbreviations and euphemisms that might not be familiar to the average reader.

At one time, the reporter was simply an observer, a stand-in for the reader, who told the reader what the reader herself would know if she had been present when some event transpired. In the era before radio and television, the only way one could know what the president said in a speech was to be present when he spoke and to take it down stenographically. In the newspapers of that era, a report might begin, "Today the president made the following speech to such-and-such organization in such-and-such place." And then it would print the speech verbatim.

Over time, people found this sort of literal reporting technique to be boring and pedantic, and costly in terms of column inches. Readers wanted the reporter to go through the speech and highlight the most interesting parts. They also wanted reactions to the speech and what it might mean for foreign policy, the prospects for legislation, or whatever other purpose was intended. Some papers—like the *New York Times*, which has always viewed itself as the paper of record—might still reprint an entire speech, and wire services like the Associated Press would send the text to all their subscribers. But if the average person wanted to know exactly what the president said, her options were limited.

It was essential that the reader trust the reporter to accurately quote people and that the quotes be in context and properly convey a sense of the point being made. Since readers could not confront the reporter directly to inquire about such things, they depended on editors to question reporters on their behalf. It was the editor's job to ensure accuracy, quality control, and adherence to proper journalistic methods. The editor's judgment was especially important when a source was not named, because that could indicate that the source was unreliable, possibly playing the reporter to advance her own agenda at the reader's expense.

Before the Internet, it was common for newspapers to subscribe to out-of-town papers to find out what they were saying. They also had correspondents in many cities, both foreign and domestic. Often a correspondent would simply read the local papers and then regurgitate material in a report for her own paper. Readers might not know that the reporting wasn't original because papers seldom credited out-of-town sources and only grudgingly cited crosstown rivals.

In the Internet era, it is much easier to verify information and track down the original source for reporting. Although the practice borders on plagiarism, many Internet-based publications will simply reprint material from more established publications, with credit given in an oblique or obscure way. Often a rather mundane story will be given a new headline that may or may not accurately reflect the content. This is done solely to attract clicks that translate directly into advertising dollars.

Personally, I always try to track down the original source for some story that I may consider citing or tweeting. If the source is not clearly indicated or a link is not provided, copying and pasting key phrases into a search engine will often turn it up.

As I mentioned in chapter 3, "How to Use Links," among the most frustrating journalistic conventions is the failure to give enough information so that one might locate the original source for a news story. It is very common to read, "According to a government study . . . ," which contains virtually no useful information. There are literally millions of government studies that vary tremendously in their quality and authority, and unless one at least knows the agency that produced it, finding them can be nearly impossible. One very valuable source is the little-known Federal Digital System (www.gpo.gov/fdsys), a powerful search engine that searches only federal documents.

Theoretically, a publication could simply provide a link to the study. However, in my experience many news organizations simply refuse to do so. I have also known of publications that avoid any links except to themselves, hoping to prevent readers from leaving their pages. One publication I used to write for would even change my links arbitrarily. I discovered this when I needed to refer to a document I had linked to—a speech by then Secretary of State Hillary Clinton. I had quoted her about something and provided a link directly to a transcript of the speech on the department website. But when I clicked on the link, it took me to some random story on the publication's own website that mentioned Mrs. Clinton in passing. I was infuriated and insisted that they never do this again, but I had discovered it only by accident. And I admit that I seldom check the links that editors insert into my work without telling me.

Another frustrating thing to me is that newspapers, now free from space constraints on their websites, don't do more to provide documentation and added value to their readers. For example, if a reporter conducts an interview, why publish only a few excerpts? Why not post the whole thing on the Web? Voice recognition software makes the task of transcription very easy, and readers could see for themselves whether a source is quoted accurately or in proper context. It would, if nothing else, improve credibility and accountability.

Perhaps the biggest difference between a reputable news organization and an untrustworthy one that should be shunned is whether they correct their mistakes and do so in a transparent way. Reputable publications strive to avoid mistakes by having editors who do fact checking, taking seriously reader complaints about inaccuracies, and making corrections and highlighting them. Untrustworthy ones will make statements based on the flimsiest of evidence, post material with little if any editorial oversight, and if forced to make a correction, will simply make it without alerting the reader to the fact that the text has been altered, or it may "walk back" a false statement by correcting it in future stories while leaving errors intact in earlier reports.

A quality newspaper like the *New York Times* publishes a list of corrections daily and appends the correction to the original story online so that readers will know that a correction was made. Sometimes it is a bit pedantic about such corrections, but this is an area where diligence is necessary because mistakes can take on a life of their own.

My favorite example of this involves the famous essayist H. L. Mencken. In 1917, he wrote a satirical article saying that President Millard Fillmore had installed the first White House bathtub and that the anniversary of this event ought to be remembered. The entire story was complete fiction, made up from Mencken's imagination, a point he thought was obvious. Yet subsequently, the idea that Fillmore had installed the first White House bathtub was frequently stated to be fact by various writers. Mencken was appalled, and on numerous occasions said publicly that his story was an invention, a hoax, yet until the end of his life he continued to come across references to Fillmore's first-ever White House bathtub as if it were common knowledge. I have seen them myself.

The problem has gotten much worse in the Internet era, for at least two reasons. One is the speed at which a lie or an error can travel. The other is the proliferation of satirical websites and the propensity of people to use sarcasm as a way of putting down political opponents. The problem arises when politicians say things that sound like satire but that they actually believe. A well-known satirical publication is *The Onion*. When I write about something silly that a politician really said, which might be mistaken for satire, I will preface it by saying, "Not from *The Onion*."

6

TRUSTING ACADEMIC SOURCES

KEY POINTS:

- Academic sources of information tend to be more trustworthy because of peer review.

- Not all academic sources are equal; universities are better than think tanks.

- There are reliable sources for good-quality policy research.

One problem every reader has these days is figuring out who to trust as an analyst or news source. It sometimes seems as if everyone is compromised, saying what is in their own economic interest or whatever suits their partisan point of view at that particular moment. Cable television is very much at fault here because it pretends that there are only two points of view on any given subject, and it seldom subjects its talking heads to much in the way of vetting.

I know that when cable news became ubiquitous in the 1990s and I was working for a conservative think tank, I would usually be paired with someone from a liberal think tank such as Brookings. The problem, from the producer's point of view, is that there were no fireworks. We usually agreed on the facts and which points of view were not supported by economic theory. So our differences on the issues tended to be nuanced, rather than stark.

As time went by, I noticed that I was less and less often paired with a think tank scholar and more and more often found myself debating someone from an activist group or a political consultant. These people had no substantive knowledge of the subjects under

THE TRUTH MATTERS

discussion. They were there to repeat talking points and that's all. Sometimes I would search their names on the Internet afterward and could find absolutely nothing about them. They were so obscure it was as if they didn't exist at all.

The final straw for me was when I went on some program to debate the minimum wage and I was put up against an honest-to-God homeless person complete with a shopping cart full of his worldly possessions. I never went on that network again. Not surprisingly, it went out of business.

The point is that one cannot necessarily trust those anointed as "experts" on cable news or even in quality newspapers to really be experts on the subjects they are talking about. Even those who at least have degrees in the subjects they opine about may not be up to speed on the latest research, or their area of specialization may be well outside the area they are being quoted on.

Of course, the average person can't be expected to necessarily know who is a genuine expert and who isn't. But consumers do need to be skeptical whenever someone doesn't appear to be affiliated with a reputable institution or lacks reasonable experience, such as a high-level government position, in their supposed area of expertise. Nevertheless, there are a few guidelines that I use myself to figure out who is reputable and who isn't.

Personally, I rely on genuine academics—professors at major universities. Aside from the obvious fact that they really are the experts, university professors have reputations to maintain that they safeguard zealously. They are also accustomed to peer pressure from their departments and universities to avoid saying something that would cause them embarrassment by being wrong or far from the mainstream of academic opinion.

At one time, getting the academic point of view on some subject was prohibitively difficult. Academics were discouraged from offering their views except in densely written and extremely obscure journals filled with incomprehensible jargon. But one could reasonably trust information that appeared in such publications because they have to undergo peer review in order to be published. Typically, two blind reviewers unknown to the author (and who don't know the author) would have to certify that the facts and methodology were sound before an article could be published.

But today, most universities encourage their professors to be more active in engaging the public in their research through interviews and op-ed articles. Virtually all top academics now have web pages where one can find their publications and research interests. The History News Network (historynewsnetwork .org) is a site where professional historians comment on current policy issues from a historical perspective. The *Washington Post* maintains a page called the "Monkey Cage" (www.washingtonpost .com/news/monkey-cage) where political scientists discuss politics in an accessible but academically rigorous way. Science News (www.sciencenews.org) is a good source for news in that field. The National Bureau of Economic Research (www.nber.org) posts cutting-edge economic research, hot off the press, in the form of working papers that can be purchased for just $5.

One way to find academic research is by using Google Scholar (scholar.google.com). This is a specialized search engine that searches only academic publications. When one searches a term such as "tax reform," the top research that comes up is by scholars I know to be experts in this field. Thus I know that when I see these scholars cited in news reports I can reasonably trust what they have to say.

Google Scholar often links to versions of academic studies that are freely available in either published form or a working paper version. These days, almost all such studies have executive summaries that tell you as much as you need to know about their findings. If you want the complete study you can either consult your local library (see chapter 7) or subscribe to a service called JSTOR, which has hundreds of academic journals available to be read online. For $200 per year you can download copies for your personal use—a very thrifty alternative, considering that many academic journals charge that much or more for an annual subscription.

JSTOR also has a blog that comments on issues of the day and cites academic research on them with free copies of the articles that are referenced at daily.jstor.org. The Oxford University Press (blog .oup.com) does something similar. I have both in my RSS reader (see chapter 13). The Shorenstein Center at Harvard University maintains a site called Journalist's Resource (journalistsresource.org) that calls attention to recent academic research on subjects of topical interest.

Back when academic research was far less accessible than it is today, think tanks served as a sort of middle-person. People at these institutions would study the academic research and talk to university professors about their research. They would then translate it into terms the average policymaker could understand and relate it to issues being discussed in Congress. Such analyses were also very helpful to reporters looking for ways to summarize academic research in ways comprehensible to average people.

Unfortunately, think tanks have since become highly politicized, and most are not very trustworthy anymore. I seldom utilize them unless I am looking for the line of the day on some topic. For example, the Heritage Foundation often establishes the conservative position on issues well before they become topics of media or congressional attention.

Few people know that all tax-exempt organizations, including think tanks, must file tax returns using IRS Form 990. By law, these forms must be made public.

They often contain useful information about the salaries of top executives, the percentage of funds that go into operations versus administrative overhead, and so on. An organization called Guidestar (www .guidestar.org) compiles filings of Form 990 and other public information that can easily be downloaded.

One source I use extensively that is reputable, unbiased, and relatively accessible is the Congressional Research Service (CRS). It is a sort of think tank for Congress itself that digests various topics and issues reports that are authoritative without being pedantic. The problem with CRS reports is that the general public cannot access them directly; they are only available through members of Congress. However, there are two private sites that try to get all of them and make them available: the Federation of American Scientists site (fas.org/sgp/crs) and Every CRS Report (www.everycrsreport.com). I highly recommend CRS reports for those seeking an unbiased, authoritative, and reasonably accessible summary and analysis of some topic of current interest, such as health reform or tax reform.

7

WHAT YOUR LOCAL LIBRARY HAS TO OFFER IN TERMS OF NEWS

KEY POINTS:

- Libraries are even more essential in the Internet era; they are the gatekeepers of trustworthy information.

- Virtually all public libraries allow free online access to extremely valuable news and research databases.

- Search engines of major newspapers are invaluable.

It may seem to you that libraries have become somewhat anachronistic in the Internet era. Today, many people ask why you would go there to look up information in dusty books when a simple Internet search will tell you whatever you want to know.

While books may not be the essential sources of basic information that they were historically, libraries today are much more than just book collections. Many local libraries now have online databases available free to anyone with a library card. State libraries may have additional databases available, and even top university libraries are often accessible to their alumni.

My personal experience is with the Fairfax County library in Virginia, where I live. On the library home page is a link to online resources. There are a number of databases listed to help people with a variety of things, such as personal investments, genealogy, and even auto repairs. I will concentrate here on those dealing with news.

One of the most powerful is called ProQuest. You click the icon and are asked for your library card number; if you don't have one, you can probably apply online. This will bring you to a typical search engine that will search the thousands of publications it has indexed. Many have full text access, although some academic publications may have what's called a "moving wall," meaning that full access may be limited to only those articles published over a year ago.

Insofar as news is concerned, I have full access to the *New York Times, Wall Street Journal, Washington Post,* and *Los Angeles Times.* The availability of particular newspapers varies according to your library's contract with ProQuest. But the *Times* and the *Journal* are true national newspapers that are very widely available on library websites.

This is important, of course, because both the *Times* and *Journal* require subscriptions for full access to their articles; only a very limited number are available to nonsubscribers, and access may also require registering with the paper and getting a username and password. As this is written, a basic online subscription to the *Times* costs $15 per month or $180 per year; one for the *Journal* is close to $400 per year after an introductory discount rate.

These rates are obviously well beyond the means of most Americans. Yet on their local library website they may be available for free. Admittedly, ProQuest's online offering is not as easy to read as a traditional newspaper's print edition or even its web page. But it is there for those looking for something in particular. I often copy and paste the headline from the *Wall Street Journal*, to which I don't subscribe, into ProQuest to call up a free copy of that article.

In one respect ProQuest has a search engine superior to the *Times'* own search engine for searching its archives. If you have only a vague sense of when some article appeared and have a mass of citations to search, ProQuest will give you a graph showing the distribution of when articles began appearing and their frequency distribution. I find this very helpful in sorting search results and homing in on precisely what I am looking for.

According to the American Library Association, EBSCO Information Services and Gale are two other databases widely available on library websites that also have access to a number of news publications. They really aren't set up to allow a user to simply scan or browse a particular publication, and full text availability is sometimes very limited. But they have search engines and access to many publications that would never turn up or would be unavailable to read in a general Internet search engine such as Google or Yahoo.

If you're a college graduate looking for more advanced library access, check with the school you went to. Many offer alumni some access to the university's online subscriptions. You will have to register as an alumnus first and be given a university ID or email address to use for access.

I went to Georgetown University and they have a number of databases available, including ProQuest. But because the university's contract with ProQuest is different than Fairfax County's, there are newspapers and other publications available here that aren't available on the Fairfax version. Georgetown also allows alumni access to other useful databases, such as *Congressional Quarterly,* which is invaluable for research on laws and public policy, and to a number of academic journals that would be prohibitively expensive for an individual to subscribe to through databases such as Project Muse.

8

NUMBERS MUST BE PUT INTO CONTEXT

KEY POINTS:

- Price data from the past needs to be routinely adjusted for inflation.

- Large numbers, such as the federal budget, are often best expressed as percentages of GDP.

- Caution is advised when using rates of change, which can exaggerate real phenomena.

Among my pet peeves are articles that reference prices from the distant past that are not adjusted for inflation. It tells a reader nothing to say that the price of some product was X thousand dollars in the 1950s and has risen to XX thousand dollars today. During that time period, the general price level has risen considerably, as have wages and incomes. What people generally want to know is how much the price of that good has increased in real or inflation-adjusted terms. Only then can they tell whether the product has become more expensive in a meaningful sense.

Perhaps at one time a reporter writing on deadline could be excused for not calculating the real price change when referencing figures from the past. But today it is very easy. The Bureau of Labor Statistics (BLS), which determines the Consumer Price Index, has an easy-to-use calculator at data.bls.gov/cgi-bin/cpicalc.pl. Or one can search the term "CPI Inflation Calculator" and it should be the first thing that pops up.

You put a price—say, $10,000 in 1960—into the calculator and it will tell you that $10,000 in 1960 is roughly equivalent to $82,000 in 2017. In other words, the general price level rose more than eight times between 1960 and 2017.

Whether the standard of living has risen over that period depends on what happened to wages. If wage rates have risen less than eight times, then workers were worse off; their standard of living has fallen. If they have risen more than eight times, then their standard of living has increased.

The CPI is one of several inflation indexes collected by the federal government for different purposes. It is based on a survey conducted monthly by BLS staff, who go to stores to see what things actually sell for. The CPI is, of course, an average; some prices may be rising while others are falling. For example, computer prices tend to fall over time, offsetting the rise in prices for other things. Of course, how you are personally affected will depend on what you consume. Sometimes food prices are rising while gasoline prices are falling. If one member of a family buys the food while the other fills the tank, they may have very different impressions of the changing cost of living.

The Federal Reserve Bank of Atlanta actually has an inflation calculator that you can adjust for your own personal consumption in order to determine your own inflation rate, at www.frbatlanta.org/research/inflationproject/mycpi.aspx. Or you can search the term "MyCPI" (all one word).

There is another inflation calculator that I sometimes use, constructed by economic historians, called "Measuring Worth" (www.measuringworth.com/calculators/uscompare). It provides a variety of ways to look at changing prices in relative terms that may more meaningfully convey their impact. For example, you can compare price changes to changes in wage rates to see if the standard of living has changed.

When looking at historical living standards, keep in mind that there has been real improvement in the standard of living over time. Simply adjusting prices from the distant past for inflation, therefore, will not properly convey the degree to which people are better or worse off. Even the ultrawealthy of the past lacked things that the poor commonly own today, such as telephones, refrigerators, and air-conditioning.

Remember too that the mix of consumption has changed radically over time. People used to spend far more of their income on food than they do today;

that money has largely gone into housing, which costs much more than in the past.

Some people are reluctant to use price indexes to put the cost of goods and services into historical perspective because they believe they are deeply flawed. I suspect that most people believe the CPI understates the true rate of inflation. But most economists believe it is more likely the opposite—that it overstates inflation, because the BLS has great difficulty incorporating new products and technology into its price calculations. Quality improvements are also a problem.

Some years ago a friend of mine who worked at BLS explained this dilemma to me with an example. In the early 1970s, the government mandated that cars couldn't be started unless the seat belt was buckled. Because inflation was a big problem at the time, the agency was reluctant to add the cost of this mandate to the CPI. So it concluded that it was an improvement in quality, on the theory that if a price rises 10 percent and the product's quality also rises 10 percent, there is no inflation.

The problem was, people hated this mandate, and it was soon repealed. So now BLS had to figure out how to incorporate this into the CPI. Since the increase in cost had been disregarded, it had to find some way of disregarding the cost of eliminating the mandate without corrupting the CPI. So BLS concluded that *eliminating* the seat belt mandate was also a quality improvement! The CPI went back to what it was before the mandate was enacted.

If you are dealing with very large numbers, such as the budget deficit, the best way to put them into context is to calculate them as a percentage of the gross domestic product (GDP), which is the dollar value of all economic transactions in the economy. It consists of all consumption by households and governments plus all investment by businesses and government minus the trade deficit (exports minus imports). Official GDP data since 1929 is calculated by a government agency, the Bureau of Economic Analysis, and economic historians have calculated it back to the eighteenth century. The Measuring Worth website will calculate any number as a share of GDP.

When comparing price or other economic data between countries, obviously we need to adjust for the exchange rate of different currencies. These numbers change daily, and many people will simply use the latest figure to put foreign data into dollar terms. For example, as this is written a British pound is worth US$1.20. Conversely, US$1 is worth eight-tenths of a pound, so US$100 is worth £80.

However, economists generally avoid making comparisons between countries based on market exchange rates, because they can convey a false impression. If the dollar rises 5 percent against the pound, Americans don't suddenly become 5 percent richer than people living in Britain, and those in Britain didn't suddenly get 5 percent poorer. But that result is strongly implied by using market exchange rates to calculate comparative costs of living.

Instead, economists use the theory of *purchasing power parity* (PPP) to make cross-country price comparisons. It's not really important to know how PPP is calculated by international organizations, such as the Organization for Economic Cooperation and Development. The average person needs to know only that it is generally wrong to use market exchange rates, and when reading about the standard of living in some other country compared to the United States, it is essential that the figures be converted using PPP.

Sometimes you need to see numbers expressed graphically to understand their significance. Fortunately, there an easy way to do this: the Federal Reserve Bank of St. Louis maintains a website called FRED (for Federal Reserve economic data; fred.stlouisfed .org) that does this easily. Thousands of economic statistics are available that can be graphed in nominal terms or inflation-adjusted terms, or as rates of change.

Incidentally, one must be careful when using rates of change. If the starting base is very low, then even a very small change may appear deceptively large. For example, the incidence of a disease might be 1 case per 100,000 population. If it rises to 2 cases, one could accurately say that the chance of catching this disease has doubled, which may sound frightening unless you know that it has risen from 1 case per 100,000 (extremely rare) to just 2 (still extremely rare).

Another source of confusion arises from using an average or mean figure when the median may better convey what is happening. The mean is simply the arithmetic sum of figures in a data set divided by the number of observations. The average income of a population would be the sum of the incomes of all people in that population divided by the number of people. This figure would also be the income per capita.

However, the average income may not accurately convey how well the population is doing if the distribution is highly unequal—a few very rich people may pull up the average, thus making the average person appear better off than she is. In this case, the median may be a better figure to use. The median is the exact middle of the distribution—for the median income, half of the population would make more and half would make less.

It is a banal but true observation that figures don't lie, but liars figure. It is easy to be misled by many forms of data. There are so many ways of distorting them to make some point that even top academics can be misled. The best advice? Be skeptical, and don't be afraid to question a source or demand better context.

9

BEWARE OF DECEPTIVE LABELING

KEY POINTS:

- The terms "right" and "left" have changed over time.

- Be aware of the "Overton window."

- The media is often guilty of treating issues as if there were only two sides.

The mainstream media is loath to quote people without telling readers something about where that person is coming from, so that they have some idea of the source's credibility or biases. But too often, the labels commonly used to describe people and organizations obfuscate more than they illuminate.

A favorite media term is "nonpartisan." The Congressional Budget Office is nearly always described this way. While the CBO is a fine organization that generally strives for objectivity, it is not altogether nonpartisan. It is, after all, a part of the legislative branch subject to political pressure. Its director is appointed by the majority party, and both sides try to appoint directors who are sympathetic to their philosophy within the bounds of economic science and generally accepted analytical methods.

While "nonpartisan" simply means not formally aligned with a particular political party, it is sometimes misused to imply objectivity. When a reporter cites a nonpartisan study, she implies that it can be taken as truthful, which may or may not be the case. Some self-proclaimed nonpartisan organizations are highly ideological and may be closely allied with a political party, claiming nonpartisanship simply to protect their tax-exempt status or as PR to gain more media traction for their point of view.

Perhaps the biggest problem with media labeling is its convention of treating every issue as if there are two and only two sides to it—the right/conservative/ Republican side and the left/liberal/Democratic side. Nuanced views that don't fit neatly into one box or the other tend to be ignored. The only exception is that those in the media are permitted to say "a pox on both your houses" and say that both sides are equally wrong about some piece of conventional wisdom.

In most cases, both-siderism is just an excuse to avoid taking sides, rather than a writer using her judgment and analysis to say one side is for the most part right and the other mostly wrong. The worst aspect of both-siderism to me is when one side's very mild offense is equated with the other side's capital offense; for example, when a little white lie about nothing important and the other side's big whopper about something important are condemned equally as lies.

Another problem is that media shorthand has great difficulty conveying the changing nature of philosophical or political points of view. The Republican Party has long been the right-of-center or conservative party and the Democrats have been the left-of-center liberal or progressive party. But most political scientists recognize that both parties have moved further toward their respective poles over the last couple of decades. That is to say, the parties have become more polarized over time.

The reasons for this polarization are many and complex. But one cause must certainly be the propensity of people to get their news from politically and philosophically compatible sources. Even if those sources present only accurate, truthful information, the way they present it, the decision to emphasize certain stories while ignoring others—these will affect how people think about the news. Simply changing the order in which certain stories are presented or how much time or space is devoted to them can easily bias the way they are perceived, even if all the facts are absolutely accurate.

For many years, the journalistic ideal was to get as close to objectivity as humanly possible. But many people argued that this was an unattainable goal that glossed over implicit biases. In some cases, this was probably a good thing. In the 1960s, the mainstream media was committed to the civil rights struggle. It would have been grotesque to treat racism and forced segregation as if they were legitimate points of view that deserved equal time.

Of course, few issues are as clear-cut as civil rights. Most issues these days don't fall as neatly on the scale of right and wrong. There is also the unfortunate tendency of the two major parties to be rank hypocrites about various issues depending on whether they are in power or not. Republicans tend to be very concerned about the budget deficit when they are out of power, not so much when they are in power. Conversely, Democrats are more suspicious of the military when they are out of power than when they are in power.

The effect of polarization makes it harder for the media to accurately characterize the philosophical leanings of the two parties. One way of describing this problem is called the "Overton window" (or "window of discourse"). Think of looking out an actual window— you can see only what the window frame allows you to see, which may be a limited view of a large expanse.

If the window moves, you may be looking at the same expanse, but your perspective has now changed. If you are not conscious that the window has moved, you may be misled into thinking that your change in what you can see represents a fundamental change rather than simply a change in perspective. For example, it used to be socially unacceptable to show black people and white people in romantic relationships together. Now it is common to see such relationships on television and in movies. The Overton window shifted toward acceptance of a phenomenon that was always there but previously ignored or avoided.

This problem is compounded by the desire of partisans to maintain a linkage to their past and to pretend, in many cases, that their ideology is unchanged when in fact it has moved sharply to the right or left. Republicans will always claim that their policies are consistent with those of Ronald Reagan, because he is viewed as a successful president who implemented Republican policies that helped the American people. Democrats feel the same way about Franklin D. Roosevelt.

But Republican policies today have little in common with Reagan's, and Democratic policies have little in common with FDR's. It can hardly be otherwise. Circumstances have changed, as have the nature of the problems government must cope with. Moreover, the policy successes and failures of the past have changed the policy landscape. We are a different country today because of programs, like Social Security, that FDR enacted, and the tax policies that Reagan enacted, as well the highly articulate ways in which they explained and justified their respective philosophies. The bully pulpit is a critical part of a president's power.

Confusion is probably greatest when discussing factions within the two parties. Because it is a familiar framework, these factions are often characterized as "right" and "left" even though the terms lack meaning in this context. As is well known, for many years there were many objective conservatives, mostly in the South, in the Democratic Party, and many objective liberals, mostly from the Northeast, in the GOP. But over the last few decades, all the conservatives in the Democratic Party joined the Republican Party and all the Republican Party's liberals became Democrats. It is confusing to news consumers when debates among Democratic liberals are mischaracterized as between right and left wings of the party. Similarly, it's confusing when debates among Republican conservatives are said to pit those on the right against others on the left. The differences are often tactical rather than philosophical.

There is no easy answer to the problem of simplistic labeling. Reporters need to stop assuming that every political fight somehow or other pits a group on the right against a symmetrical group on the left. It's lazy to use such terms instead of making the effort to lay out the differences in more concrete detail. News consumers need to be conscious of the Overton window—the movable frame through which they view the two parties and the ideological movements associated with them. Polarization is a fact of life that makes comparisons between the ideological foundations of the parties today and those in the past highly tenuous in many cases.

10

THE PERILS OF POLLING

KEY POINTS:

- Polls are easily manipulated, but polling is still a valid statistical tool.

- Samples must be random to be valid, but weighting can undermine validity.

- It's best to look at trends and confirmation of results by different pollsters.

Public opinion polling has become ubiquitous; it's a rare day that some major new poll isn't released, with important political implications. While it's always useful to know what average people think, polls are not benign. They can create bandwagon effects so that people may feel compelled to go along with the crowd on some issue despite having serious misgivings.

Poll results can also easily be slanted. This fact is often obvious when one reads the actual wording of a poll, which may lend itself too easily to a particular response. Clever pollsters can bias their results more subtly by putting questions into a particular order or making certain adjustments to the results.

As everyone knows, polls are based on samples. It would be prohibitively expensive to ask every American their opinion on some subject. The decennial census comes close to doing this, and it costs billions of dollars to conduct. In contrast, a typical national poll will interview about 1,500 people.

Many people are inherently skeptical of polling, believing it impossible to validly infer the opinions of hundreds of millions of people from such a small sample. But long experience shows that this can be done;

indeed, businesses use sampling techniques every day to ensure quality control of their products. Rather than test all of them, they test a representative sample.

The key to whether a sample is indeed representative and unbiased is whether it is random. This is hard to achieve and often requires some adjustment to the results. For example, suppose you know that a certain population is exactly 50 percent men and 50 percent women, and gender is potentially an important factor. If you sample one hundred people and find that sixty of the responses are from men and only forty from women, you have a biased sample.

You could keep polling until you get a 50-50 sample. But polling is expensive; it typically involves phoning people and asking them questions. And a polling company may need to place many calls before finding someone willing to answer its questions. To save on costs, therefore, pollsters simply inflate the population underrepresented in the sample and deflate the one that is oversampled.

In this example, a pollster would multiply each female result by 1.25 so that the forty women who responded would carry a weight of fifty in the results.

Conversely, the male sample would by multiplied by .833 so that the sixty responses from them would also carry a weight of fifty in the results. Thus each response is adjusted so that the final weighting of the sample equals that of the population you are studying.

Incidentally, this shows how critical census data is to pollsters. They must have some objective criteria about a given population or their adjustments will be invalid and possibly bias the results.

Depending on what subject you are polling, many adjustments may need to be made to the sample for age, race, geography, income, and political party. The last is important in predicting election results. But it's not enough to just know how many Republicans and Democrats are in an area being polled. You also need to know whether they are registered, because non-registered people can't vote. And you need to know the propensity of a voter to actually vote. Experience will tell a pollster what characteristics separate a likely voter from an unlikely one, and every pollster does it differently, which is one reason why results differ.

In the early days of polling, it was so extraordinarily expensive and time-consuming that there were only a couple of national polls during an entire election cycle. Politicians depended more on informal polling—checking in with precinct captains who kept their ears to the ground, gauging the size and intensity of crowds for appearances, and so on. This worked well enough when the population was much smaller and suffrage was limited to property-owning white males. But today all candidates for major offices poll as often as they can—even daily, if they can afford it.

Fortunately, the cost of polling has fallen as automated phone systems and online polling methods have become common. But this also means that there are more fly-by-night polling firms out there willing to cut corners to give the person paying for the poll the answer they want. Indeed, some polling firms don't actually poll at all; they conduct what are called push polls. Under the guise of asking someone their opinion, they give them a sales pitch, which is the actual purpose of the call.

It is difficult to know which polls to trust. People have a natural tendency to trust those that show their candidate or cause winning and to distrust those that don't. The best way to get the unvarnished truth from polling is to look at a range of polls from different poll-sters, look at the trend of polls, and dismiss outliers. An outlier is simply a result far out of line with other polls. It's like flipping a coin and getting heads ten times in a row. It would be foolish to think that the next ten coin flips will also be heads, so you ignore that result.

Fortunately, there are websites that aggregate and compile a variety of polls. One that I find useful is from a site called RealClearPolitics (www.realclearpolitics .com/epolls/latest_polls). Updated daily, it shows all the polls released that day on subjects such as approval of the president and Congress, direction of the country, and support for legislative initiatives.

Another polling site I use is PollingReport.com. It is a more issue-oriented site that lets you see the latest polling on issues like gun control, immigration, tax reform, and whatever else is in the news that pollsters have questioned people about. The gold standard in terms of issue polling is the Pew Research Center, which funds its own polling and is not beholden to those commissioning a poll.

One way of determining whether a poll is repu-table is to see whether it adheres to the standards of the American Association for Public Opinion Research. Among the ethical standards are full disclosure of who pays for a poll, transparent methodologies, and so on. Generally speaking, polls commissioned by major news organizations, such as the *New York Times,* Associated Press, or the major television news organizations, can be trusted to adhere to the ethical standards of proper polling.

Given that most major pollsters have websites these days, it is a simple matter to go to them and download a complete poll, rather than rely on a reporter's summary, which may only highlight a couple of questions. In my experience, the vast majority of poll results that are publicly available are never reported in the media. This is too bad, because I often find very interesting tidbits of information buried in the details.

Perhaps the biggest myth of polling is that public opinion is relatively fixed. But of course it changes; indeed, the whole point of advertising and political campaigns is to change public opinion. Pollsters also know that as an election gets closer, people pay closer attention to the candidates and may change their minds in rapid succession. That's one reason why polls vary and is just part of the polling process.

It's understood, but nevertheless must be repeated: even the best polls are just snapshots of what people are thinking at a given moment in time. It may or may not tell you what will happen on Election Day or at some point in the future. And as we know from the 2016 election, even when national polls are accurate, they don't necessarily forecast the winner. Virtually all the pollsters projected that Hillary Clinton would win the national popular vote, and she did. But presidential elections are determined by winning electoral votes, which means carrying a combination of specific states. Donald Trump carried more states and got more electoral votes, which won him the White House despite losing the popular vote by a fairly large margin.

The best advice is to be skeptical of all polls—especially when they confirm your own beliefs. Try to look at a range of polls and the trend lines. Be more skeptical of polls early in the electoral process; pay attention to who is paying for a poll and whether they have an ax to grind. A poll from the National Republican Congressional Committee is going to be biased in favor of GOP candidates, in order to help fund-raising and morale. So if it shows the Republican just barely ahead, she's probably running behind.

Finally, be aware that it is very hard to poll intensity of opinion. On a snowy day in November, the more committed voters will find a way to vote, and the candidate who would win easily on a sunny day may find herself the loser.

11

USING WIKIPEDIA

KEY POINTS:

- Wikipedia is a very powerful but deeply flawed research tool.

- Wikipedia is a great place to start research and a terrible place to end it.

- It's well worth learning how to search the Internet effectively.

Wikipedia is simultaneously one of the most wonderful reference sources ever invented, a true gift of the Internet era, and also one of the most frustrating and easily misused.

At the risk of belaboring the obvious, I must caution that Wikipedia is not always a dependable source, and much of what appears there is not necessarily accurate. But it depends a lot on the nature of the subject one is researching.

In all my years of using Wikipedia, I don't think I have ever been misled about a basic historical fact, such as when someone was born or where or other standard biographical information. I find it most useful as a place to start when I want to learn about a subject I know nothing about. Let me repeat—*a place to start*. You never want to finish your research on Wikipedia.

Where Wikipedia is more problematic is when dealing with hot, current topics. Both the great strength and the great weakness of Wikipedia is that volunteers write almost all of it and anyone can initiate or edit an entry, subject to verification by Wikipedia editors and possibly the conflicting views of other volunteers.

Sometimes contributors abuse Wikipedia or try to impose a particular point of view on contentious issues. Politicians have been known to have their staffs repeatedly edit certain material in or out, and Wikipedia must sometimes take action to prevent this.

The best thing about Wikipedia to me is the reference material. Sometimes all I need is the name of one good book or article on a subject to begin my research, but I don't know where to start. If I have even a single reference, I can plug it into Google Scholar and see whether it has been widely referenced—an important clue to its standing and reliability on the subject—and find other books and articles on the same subject.

Sometimes the authors of Wikipedia entries are people with inside knowledge of the subject they are writing about. For example, many years ago I started my own Wikipedia entry with a bit of information about my life and work. For quite a few years now, it has been the very first thing that turns up when someone searches my name in Google or some other search engine.

But I confess that I have not looked at my entry for a long time. I once looked at it, found that some inaccuracy had crept in, and attempted to fix it. A Wikipedia editor asked me for documentation before allowing the change to take effect. I said the documentation is that I am me and I know that what was written was wrong. The editor told me that wasn't good enough. Lacking documentation that I could link to, I gave up my effort to fix my own Wikipedia entry and have not looked at it since. I have no idea whether the inaccuracy I attempted to fix is still there or not.

To me, this is a cautionary tale about the risk of relying on Wikipedia. Nevertheless, I assume that someone who knows nothing about me will find a few things that are accurate—jobs I've held, books I've written, and so on—that would inform them about other places to look for information about me that are in fact reliable.

It helps if one thinks of Wikipedia as simply the latest version of an old standby, the encyclopedia. When I was a child, every family had one. Salesmen would sell them door to door, and supermarkets might run weekly specials of one volume for a very low price to lure shoppers into the store. The biggest problem with the encyclopedia was that much of it rapidly went out of date, and the brevity of the entries often made them of little value. But like Wikipedia, they were usually a good place to start one's research on some topic one knew nothing about.

The next step—then and, as it should be, today—is the local library. The amount of material available on my local library's website is vast and includes reputable encyclopedias, written, curated, and edited by professional experts. And unlike the encyclopedias of old, they are continuously kept up to date.

One trick I use to determine the usefulness of a reference source is to search a topic I already know a bit about. Its discussion of that topic will usually tell me right away whether it is thorough or superficial, biased or objective, slipshod or dependable. I know that if the discussion I am familiar with is reliable, I can usually depend on subjects I am not familiar with to be reliable as well.

Armed with a few basic facts and references, it is now much easier to use a general search engine to find out what one wants to know and separate the wheat from the chaff. As everyone knows, one of the most difficult things to do when searching the Internet is finding the right search terms to use. You wouldn't look for a restaurant in your neighborhood or town by just searching the term "restaurants" in Google. That would turn up far too many places to do you any good.

Obviously, to find what you are looking for you must limit your search. By now, most people have at least some familiarity with Boolean search techniques—using the words "and," "or," and "not" to include or exclude certain results. Most people also probably know to put terms into quotation marks so that exact term will be searched and not just the individual words. But there are a great many other search techniques. For those looking for a list of search methods to help them find exactly what they are looking for on a particular website or across the Internet, I recommend www .googleguide.com.

Keep in mind that a vast amount of material will never turn up using a general search engine like Google, which tends to skim the surface. Those wishing to go deeper may want to use the so-called wayback machine at archive.org, which attempts to archive everything on the Internet, including pages that have disappeared from their original sites.

Personally, I like searching for information through a reputable newspaper such as the *New York Times*, which is probably available for free through your local library's website. Another method is to use Google's newspaper archives at news.google.com/newspapers.

12

THE PROBLEM OF FAKE NEWS

KEY POINTS:

- What is fake news?

- What is fact checking?

- How has the journalistic demand for access to sources undermined routine fact checking?

"Fake news" is a term that has come into common currency since the election of Donald Trump. According to Google Trends, interest in it suddenly took a big jump right around Election Day 2016.

Originally, fake news referred to satirical news of the sort that appeared on *The Daily Show* or *The Colbert Report*. More recently, President Trump has used the term as an accusation against news organizations reporting accurate news that he doesn't like.

Fake news is an odd term that seemingly connotes two related but different ideas. One is more akin to pseudo news—stories that aren't really newsworthy but are nevertheless presented as such. A lot of celebrity gossip falls into this category. The other sense of fake news is the presentation of falsehoods as if they are in fact true.

Most people's main concern about fake news is its role in the political process, which dates back to the nation's origins. Ben Franklin was among those who practiced the art of political deception, publishing a counterfeit newspaper to mislead the British public and create sympathy for the new American republic during diplomatic negotiations. Printing outright lies about one's political opponents was a mainstay of campaigning throughout the nineteenth century.

If the concept of fake news is not new, its current techniques are. The Internet and social media have made it very easy to peddle and promote lies. Although theoretically these same methods ought to enable truth to win out in the end, in practice this has proven not to be the case. Political scientists have found that when people who have been exposed to lies are confronted with the truth, they often believe the lie even more strongly. One reason is that simple repetition of a lie, even in the course of refuting it, lends it credibility. Another reason is confirmation bias—people believe what they want to believe.

Sadly, there are a number of popular websites, publications, and radio hosts who appear to just literally make things up and knowingly present lies as truth in order to make money or to promote an ideological or partisan agenda. A lot of Americans, it seems, believe crazy conspiracy theories about a wide range of subjects and cannot be dissuaded from them. And experience shows that belief in one conspiracy theory tends to lead people to believe other, unrelated conspiracy theories as well.

News organizations have responded by setting up fact-checking operations. The *Washington Post* assigned one of its most senior reporters, Glenn Kessler, to examine and report on statements by politicians that skirt the line between "truthiness," a term popularized by the comedian Stephen Colbert, and outright lies. Other organizations, such as Politifact (www.politifact.com) and FactCheck (www.factcheck .org), do something similar. The granddaddy of fact-checking sites is Snopes (www.snopes.com), which started out as someone's hobby of looking into urban legends. Its reports examine all manner of stories, from the serious to the amusing, but in a way that is both authoritative and entertaining.

While fact checking is all to the good, my problem with it is that it shouldn't be considered a separate journalistic function, but rather the core function of all journalism. If reporters and editors aren't routinely fact checking everything they publish, what the heck are they doing instead?

In the view of many critics of modern political journalism, the problem is that many reporters appear to be little more than stenographers, taking down whatever their sources tell them without subjecting their claims to scrutiny. This criticism is true, to some extent, and the blame lies with changing technology that allows politicians to bypass the mainstream media to get their message out.

When I first began working in politics in the 1970s, reporters for major newspapers like the *New York Times* were gatekeepers. You had to go through them to get publicity for whatever you were doing, because methods like paid advertising and direct mail were prohibitively expensive and not very efficient. You had to earn a reporter's trust and convince him you weren't a crackpot if you hoped to get him to report something you wanted him to write about.

C-SPAN, created in 1979, was really the first institution that changed this dynamic. Available on every cable system in the United States, it gave politicians a way to talk directly to voters without a media filter. In the 1990s, the Internet and twenty-four-hour cable news channels made it even easier for politicians to get their message out, and reporters began to lose their gatekeeper function. The economic decline of newspapers and other traditional media led to a sharp decline in both the number and the quality of reporters. Rather than take the time to thoroughly report a story, journalists are now forced to report first and ask questions later, which makes for more inaccuracies.

Knowing the enormous demand for tidbits of gossip from within the White House or a political campaign, politicians have learned to use such tidbits to get reporters to do their bidding, like dangling a carrot in front of a hungry horse to get it to pull the wagon. If a reporter writes something a politician doesn't like, she will be frozen out and a competitor will get the next scoop. Beat reporters feel it's better to just say what their sources want them to say than to risk losing access.

Unfortunately, this means that it is much easier for politicians to lie with impunity. This problem is compounded by the extreme reluctance of reporters to say that someone is lying, no matter how obvious it may be. Politicians peddle falsehoods routinely as part of their modus operandi. Whether a falsehood is a lie depends on whether someone *knows* it is a rank falsehood and falsely presents it as truth. Reporters believe that detecting this requires the ability to read minds and know a speaker's motives. They are also rightly fearful of a libel suit that could be costly and damage their reputation.

For these reasons, reporters have adopted certain conventions. One is what is called he said/she said journalism. A politician says something the reporter knows is false, but rather than say so directly the reporter will seek out a spokesman from the opposite side and quote her as saying the politician is lying. The reader is left to figure out the truth for herself and more often than not will side with whoever speaks for her side.

Of course, reporters and editors are as frustrated by this system as readers are. Fact checking has become the way they can maintain access while still being true to their journalistic principles. Someone like *Post* reporter Glenn Kessler, who doesn't cover a source directly and is therefore not dependent on access, can use his judgment to say some statement is false or even a lie. The problem is that fact checking has become a sort of journalistic ghetto. Reports that correct factual errors don't get anywhere near as much attention as breaking news does. I've never seen a fact-checking story appear on page one.

Organizations like Google and Facebook are trying to find ways to integrate fact checking into their searches and news feeds, but it is unclear whether this will cut down on the spread of falsehoods that people want to believe because it suits their partisan agenda, ideology, religion, or some other vested interest. As long as people have a strong incentive to believe a lie, liars will have an equally strong incentive to lie.

13

DESIGNING YOUR OWN NEWSPAPER

KEY POINTS:

- Technology allows you to design and customize your news sources.

- An RSS reader is useful and easy to learn.

- Twitter offers a great way to follow individual reporters you have learned to trust.

Many people continue to subscribe to a major newspaper such as the *New York Times* or *Wall Street Journal,* have the paper edition delivered to their house or office, and read it from front to back. This is still a very good way to stay informed, but one that is gradually falling out of favor. Even among those who make the effort to stay informed on the issues of the day, most now prefer to read their news online on a computer, smartphone, or other device.

Most people go to the home page of their favorite news sources to see what's new. Others may prefer a site that aggregates the news, such as Google News, where a sort of robot (algorithm) seeks out news reports and ranks them according to various criteria. Its search engine is a good way to see what a variety of news publications are reporting on some breaking story. You can personalize your news feed from Google to emphasize news on some particular topic or region of the world. You can have Google search only news sources from a particular country or region in English or other languages.

Another useful news aggregator that I rely on is RealClearPolitics (RCP; www.realclearpolitics.com).

It is curated by human beings rather than an algorithm, so its offerings are broader and more focused than those on sites curated automatically. RCP also has pages devoted to science, public policy, sports, books, and lots of other things you may wish to follow. Although not comprehensive, you are unlikely to miss anything important or about which there is "buzz."

There are many news aggregation sites, but I rely on one I have created for myself using an RSS reader. RSS stands for "rich site summary," but it is often called "really simple syndication." It is a system that uploads published material from the Internet directly to you the moment it is available. It is as if someone were reading every website you follow and letting you know the minute there is something new without your having to go to a home page and search around for it yourself.

Google once created a really excellent news reader that it later simply abandoned, to the dismay of thousands of users, me among them. Fortunately, various alternatives soon emerged. I use an RSS reader called Feedly, but there are many others to suit different devices and tastes. They all operate basically the same way. Search the term "RSS" or go to www.rss.com to find a list of various RSS readers to suit different needs and devices.

With Feedly you go to the "add content" page and type in a publication or keyword. If I search for the *New York Times,* I have a number of options. I can get all breaking news or just stories related to business, politics, or any number of other subcategories. If you click "Follow," you will begin receiving *New York Times* stories in Feedly as soon as they are posted. If you are anxious to be the first to know the news, this is a very good way to do it.

Even if you aren't especially interested in seeing stories first, RSS readers are helpful if you don't want to miss something in a favorite publication. Many people are too busy to read various publications during the week but like to catch up on weekends. If a story appeared on Monday, it has probably disappeared from the home page by Saturday. The RSS reader saves you from digging around without knowing exactly what you are looking for.

An RSS reader can also keep on top of websites that post material only very intermittently. For example, certain bloggers may post only every few months. It is frustrating to keep checking their sites for new material, not knowing when it will appear. An RSS reader will make sure you don't miss anything.

A benefit to me of using an RSS reader is the ability to follow and absorb information from literally hundreds of news sources almost simultaneously. There are probably few other people quite so obsessive, but an RSS reader doesn't necessarily have to be used to follow the sort of political and economic stories I am interested in. For example, suppose you are interested in recipes; there are dozens of sites posting new ones all the time.

Searching through Feedly's offerings on a topic such as sports may call your attention to popular sites you may not be aware of or those dedicated only to one particular sport, such as golf. A very large site such as ESPN has hundreds of thousands of followers on Feedly and will deliver well over one hundred stories a week to you if you want to make sure you don't miss anything.

Some people I know use Twitter the way I use an RSS reader. Virtually all major news outlets have Twitter feed; the one for the *New York Times* has over thirty-five million followers. One advantage is Twitter's brevity—there are no more than 140 characters in each post and usually a link directly to a *Times* report.

The problem with Twitter from my point of view is that it is not comprehensive. The *Times'* main Twitter feed posts only breaking news, although it has other feeds for politics and opinions. Twitter's advantage over an RSS reader is the option to read posts by a particular writer or reporter whom you enjoy or trust. Generally speaking, they will not only post their own work as soon as it is posted online but also post links of interest and running commentary during the day. Twitter lists seven hundred writers just from the *New York Times* with individual Twitter accounts.

The *Times'* Facebook page mirrors its Twitter feed. Although growing numbers of people use Facebook as a news source, I find it unsatisfactory for my needs. The news stories that show up in my news feed are too eclectic. I am more inclined to *post* stories on Facebook than to read them. It's a way to call interesting information to the attention of my friends, especially if it is somewhat obscure and easily overlooked.

Lastly, there are many news sites that will send you email alerts and newsletters that may recap their offerings on a daily or weekly basis. Personally, I don't like my email clogged up with such material, and signing up tends to attract spam, but this may suit the needs of some people.

The point of this discussion is that you can effectively design your own news "publication" (a sort of digest) with exactly the material you want, with whatever points of view you favor or entertain, and even highlight different reporters and writers from different publications. There is no longer any reason to rely on a one-size-fits-all format that newspapers historically have offered. Even if they achieved that goal well enough for most people in the past, they cannot do it now; their downsizing means you have to rely on a variety of news sources if you want to be well informed. Fortunately, technology makes this easy to do.

14

EDITORIAL OPINIONS

KEY POINTS:

- Newspaper editorials may have outlived their usefulness.

- Accountability and trustworthiness are better maintained when anonymity is minimized.

- Opinions aren't the same as reportage.

I think a major barrier to the credibility of media organizations, especially newspapers, is the existence of editorials. If you think about it, it's very odd that such things even exist. Why should anyone think that a brief, anonymous statement on some issue matters to anyone? It isn't as if editorial writers poll the reporters or even the other editorial writers to determine what the paper's point of view should be on a particular issue. In practice, editorial writers write brief, unsigned op-ed articles, and the head of the editorial page decides whether to publish it or not. Although theoretically editorials reflect the perspective of the owner or publisher, in practice I doubt those individuals have much to say about it, short of appointing an editorial page editor who shares their general philosophy.

I suppose there are occasions when editorials can have an impact on policy or elections, but I'm not sure I've ever seen a case. During the 2016 election, virtually every newspaper in the United States rejected Donald Trump and either stayed neutral or endorsed Hillary Clinton. Did this overwhelming editorial consensus have any impact at the polls? None that I can see.

If editorials were merely worthless remnants of an earlier era that live on because of tradition, they would be harmless. But that is not the case. First, they are not costless, in an era when newspaper budgets are severely squeezed. Big newspapers like the *New York Times* and the *Wall Street Journal* have large editorial boards that undoubtedly cost several million dollars per year to maintain. Such funds probably would be better spent on their core mission of reporting the news.

Second, in an era when newspapers have lost trust and credibility, it is a burden on the news side to prove that it is independent of its editorial philosophy. I know there are many reporters at the *Wall Street Journal,* which has a very conservative editorial page, who chafe when accused of tilting their reporting in a conservative direction or perhaps suffer some embarrassment when their stories contradict the paper's editorial line.

Although all newspapers claim to have a Great Wall between the news side and the editorial side (and the advertising side as well), I suspect that few readers believe this. It is quite reasonable for them to assume that the news coverage at a paper like the *New York Times,* with its liberal editorial position, also tilts its news in that same direction. Even if a news story is objective and truthful on some topic that the paper has strongly held views on, such as abortion or climate change, how can a reader know that inconvenient facts contrary to its editorial position weren't left out or downplayed?

Indeed, the most sophisticated argument for media bias has nothing to do with the tilting of coverage or overt expressions of opinion by reporters. It has to do with much more subtle but overarching concerns, such as *what is news*? It's reasonable to say that if you took a list of the top stories of the day and asked a group of conservatives and a group of liberals to put those stories in order of importance, the results would differ considerably in many respects.

Even in the Internet age, the decision to put a story on page one is very important at every newspaper. Historically, the story on the upper right side of the paper has been deemed to be the most important of the day. It would be naive to think that the decision to emphasize this particular item among all those available isn't influenced by the paper's political philosophy. If the placement of importance happens to align with a paper's editorial position, readers are going to suspect, rightly or wrongly, that there is a cause-and-effect relationship.

The problem, as I see it, is that editorials by their nature reflect an institutional point of view. In contrast, signed columns do not. They are the author's opinion and no one else's. Of course, the decision to run a particular columnist regularly may indicate an editorial judgment. But I know of no newspaper that runs only liberal or conservative columnists. Even the *New York Times,* probably our most liberal major newspaper, employs three conservative columnists and frequently publishes guest columns by those with a conservative point of view.

A more valid criticism of the opinions one sees on the editorial or op-ed page (which is short for opposite-the-editorial page) is that they tend to be bland and conventional. Indeed, that is the whole point of running regular columnists rather than nothing but guest columnists; the regulars are predictable, and readers know exactly what they are going to get, just as they know exactly what's on the menu when they go to McDonald's.

While writing a syndicated column for many years, I was acutely aware that I was expected to fill a certain niche, and I knew exactly who my columnist competitors were. I paid close attention to whether my subscribers actually ran a particular column and which columns appeared to be popular among the editors who decide to run mine or someone else's.

I saw that my most popular columns were always those that took a very conventional point of view, one well within the mainstream of my political orientation. My least popular columns were those where I challenged my side's ideas or positions. I'm not sure if editors were confused when I did this or if they feared that readers would be confused or alienated. In any case, it's clear that there is a strong bias on both sides of the political spectrum against columnists who buck their own side; conformity is rewarded.

Of course, the price paid is that interesting columns, columns that might make people think, tend to be rejected in favor of the boring same old, same old. There are certain well-known columnists who haven't expressed a new thought in decades yet are very widely syndicated. These two phenomena are in fact closely related.

Personally, I like having my point of view challenged and think it would benefit readers to have a wider range of opinions expressed in the limited amount of space available on a newspaper's editorial page. Although many papers now run additional columnists online, few take creative advantage of the additional space online to offer a wider range of opinions than they always have. Longtime practices die hard.

My advice is to abolish anonymous editorials altogether. Put someone's name on every opinion piece that appears. If the publisher wants to endorse a candidate, let her explain her own reasons for doing so rather than hiding behind the anonymity of an unsigned column deemed to represent the paper as a whole. Use the resources and space freed up by ending editorials to run more signed columns expressing a broader range of opinions on a wider variety of topics. Use the essentially unlimited space online to cultivate new voices and unconventional viewpoints. It costs practically nothing and may attract new readers turned off by the limited range of views currently available.

Readers should seek out such writers wherever they can be found online. Bookmark them, put them in your RSS feed, tweet and post their work on Facebook or other social media so that it reaches a broader audience. As with movies and books, word of mouth counts for a lot, and you'd be surprised how many of your friends respect your judgment that some article or columnist is worth reading. This is one way average people can make a difference. The website PunditFact (www.politifact .com/punditfact) is one place to look for truth and accuracy among opinion writers.

15

HOW TO FIGHT
FAKE NEWS

KEY POINTS:

- Critical thinking is the best defense against fake news.

- Technology may help, as may new school curricula.

- The same tools that create fake news can help fight it.

At this stage of the debate, people recognize that fake news is a problem, but the solution is elusive. Many in the tech community believe it is a problem technology can easily fix. Various efforts are under way to automatically identify fake news stories before they go viral and then either delete them from social media platforms or append some sort of warning that the story is unverifiable and possibly fake.

This is all to the good, and perhaps these automated methods will help. But I am disinclined to think they are the answer. The core problem is that people *like* fake news when it is interesting or titillating, or when it confirms a core belief—especially one that is under challenge—or scores points against a political or ideological opponent.

Even when someone is well aware of the fake news problem, the ease and simplicity with which one can repost or forward something interesting that one comes across on the Internet or in an email can overwhelm common sense for a moment, and suddenly you find that you have added to the fake news problem. I myself am guilty of tweeting such items after reading only the headline of a story that looked interesting—perhaps *too interesting*.

The fact is, there are great financial rewards to writing just the right headline to attract clicks and eyeballs. Clicks equal advertising dollars. They may also attract sponsors who pay people to generate vast numbers of posts on Twitter, Facebook, and other social media. Such methods can be nefarious, but often are simply a marketing strategy not inherently different from any other advertising or marketing effort.

Other than forcing myself to calm down, wait a moment before posting a comment, and reading a story all the way through before acting, I have found that my best defense is the old adage: If something is too good (or outrageous) to be true, it probably is. That is, try to resist gullibility and credulousness; be skeptical and agnostic until you can determine the truthfulness or validity of some news item, especially if it *confirms something you want to believe*.

Educators believe that it is up to them to teach critical thinking and drum into students certain habits that will offer some protection against being scammed by fake news themselves. They were alarmed by a 2016

Stanford University study that found that even bright, well-educated, tech-savvy students had great difficulty separating news from advertising or figuring out where a piece of information came from.

Fortunately, the same methods that allow fake news to proliferate provide the tools to fight it. One very simple method is to check whether others are reporting that too-good-to-be-true story. If your source is absolutely the only one with a particular news item, and a search through Google News or a similar source finds no confirmation, it may be that you are being scammed.

Of course, everyone likes to be the first to report some hot item to friends, and it's hard to discipline yourself to double-check an item before posting it. Sometimes you may rationalize that whether an item is true or not, it is undeniably entertaining. Thus you justify your failure to do due diligence by saying to yourself, *It's just entertainment.*

If it's a matter of no importance, you are doing no harm. Unfortunately, some very important people—anchors on cable news channels, widely syndicated talk radio hosts, and the like—use entertainment as an excuse to peddle lies. When caught, they say they are not professional journalists, but essentially entertainers. Anyway, the ultimate burden is on the reader, viewer, or listener, they say, to verify the veracity of facts; their only real job is to deliver the largest possible audience to their advertisers.

Some economists argue that competition will weed out the liars, fabulists, and propagandists. But this is rank nonsense. Competition doesn't reward the media that provides the best, most accurate reporting. Since the dawn of modern newspapers, they have strived to attract readers with a wide variety of pure entertainment—comics, gossip columns, and the like. I hardly need mention that the most popular TV news journalists all tend to be very good-looking, some exceptionally so, with pleasing voice and demeanor. Obviously, this is not coincidental.

Ethics and professional standards are one defense against fake news, but the intensity of competition has diminished their value. Indeed, there is now a sort of race to the bottom, wherein unambiguously disreputable media organizations have achieved goals unimaginable just a few years ago, such as being credentialed to the White House press corps.

This means that the burden on citizens to sift fact from fiction is getting heavier; they can no longer just assume that the gatekeepers of credible news outlets still have the power to punish the disreputable and reward accuracy and truthfulness with honors like the Pulitzer Prize. It took many years for the old practices of "yellow journalism" to be suppressed in favor of professional journalistic standards that were widely accepted.

The Center for News Literacy at Stony Brook University is in the forefront of educational efforts to fight fake news by teaching people to be discerning in their news consumption—to tell the difference between news and rumor, news and advertising, news and opinion, bias and fairness. The Center is developing a curriculum to achieve these goals; it can be either offered as stand-alone courses or integrated into existing social studies. The problem, of course, is that any time new material is introduced into a school curriculum, something else has to be dropped or cut back.

Ideally, critical thinking is a core educational function embedded into virtually every course to some extent, from kindergarten all the way up. My wife, Nancy, taught eighth-grade English at an urban middle school for seventeen years. She always thought that critical thinking, proper evaluation of source materials, and other elements of news literacy were a key part of her job, long before the fake news problem arose.

As noted earlier, it is not enough to have separate sections of a newspaper devoted to fact checking when to my mind fact checking is *the* core journalistic function. Having a separate section suggests that the rest of the paper doesn't engage in fact checking. Similarly, critical thinking is the core function of a proper educational system; teaching it in a separate course to fight the scourge of fake news should be superfluous.

It's possible that as time goes by the problem of fake news will take care of itself. It's become such an acute problem only because social networks are still relatively new and those who learned how to promote fake news in service of an agenda have a head start. Eventually people may learn to be more discriminating on their own, or the various technological fixes will be successful.

In the end, the best defenses against fake news are critical thinking; taking in news from a variety of sources, including those that don't confirm your own biases; being skeptical about information that sounds too good (or bad) to be true; and other self-defenses.

SUGGESTED RESOURCES

> **Facebook** has posted guidelines for how its users can spot fake news at www.facebook.com/help/188118808357379. Tips include being skeptical of shocking headlines, watching for unusual formatting or manipulated images, checking the timeline, and seeking confirmation in other media coverage.

BOOKS:

Brooke Borel, *The Chicago Guide to Fact-Checking*. University of Chicago Press, 2016.

Anthony Grafton, *The Footnote: A Curious History*. Harvard University Press, 1997.

Bill Kovach and Tom Rosenstiel, *Blur: How to Know What's True in the Age of Information Overload*. Bloomsbury, 2010.

Bill Kovach and Tom Rosenstiel, *The Elements of Journalism: What Newspeople Should Know and the Public Should Expect*. Three Rivers Press, 2014.

Daniel J. Levitin, *Weaponized Lies: How to Think Critically in the Post-Truth Era*. Dutton, 2017.

Farad Manjoo, *True Enough: Learning to Live in a Post-Fact Society*. John Wiley, 2008.

Richard E. Rubin, *Foundations of Library and Information Science, 4th ed.* Neal-Schuman, 2016.

Sarah Harrison Smith, *The Fact Checker's Bible: A Guide to Getting It Right.* Anchor Books, 2004.

William B. Strunk Jr. and E. B. White, *The Elements of Style, 2nd ed.* Macmillan, 1972.

RELIABLE NEWS AND STATISTICS RESOURCES:

Bureau of Labor Statistics (BLS) (data.bls.gov/cgi-bin/cpicalc.pl): Easy-to-use calculator.

Congressional Research Service (CRS): Produces digests and reports that are authoritative without being pedantic; reports are accessible at the Federation of American Scientists (fas.org/sgp/crs) and Every CRS Report (www.everycrsreport.com) sites.

Federal Reserve Bank of Atlanta (www.frbatlanta.org/research/inflationproject/mycpi.aspx): Inflation calculator customizable to an individual's consumption.

Feedly (www.rss.com): RSS reader.

FRED (Federal Reserve economic data) (fred.stlouisfed.org): Provides thousands of economic statistics that can be graphed in nominal terms or inflation-adjusted terms, or as rates of change.

Google newspaper archives (news.google.com/newspapers).

Google Scholar (scholar.google.com): Specialized search of academic publications.

Guidestar (www.guidestar.org): Compiles filings of Form 990 and other public information that can easily be downloaded.

History News Network (historynewsnetwork.org): Historical perspectives on current policy issues by professional historians.

Journalist's Resource (journalistsresource.org): Focuses on recent academic research on subjects of topical interest; maintained by the Shorenstein Center at Harvard University.

JSTOR blog (daily.jstor.org): Commentary on issues of the day, citing academic research, with free copies of referenced articles.

Measuring Worth (www.measuringworth.com/calculators/uscompare): Inflation calculator constructed by economic historians.

Monkey Cage (www.washingtonpost.com/news/monkey-cage): Accessible but academically rigorous discussion by political scientists.

National Bureau of Economic Research (www.nber.org): Cutting-edge economic research.

Oxford University Press blog (blog.oup.com): Similar to JSTOR blog.

PollingReport.com: Provides the latest polling on top issues like gun control, immigration, and tax reform.

ProQuest: Database, offered through libraries, that provides archival or full access to thousands of indexed publications.

RealClearPolitics (RCP; www.realclearpolitics.com): A useful aggregator of important news, curated by human beings, with broader and more focused offerings than those on automatically curated sites. Pages are devoted to science, public policy, sports, books, and so on.

RealClearPolitics Polls (www.realclearpolitics.com/epolls/latest_polls): Aggregates and compiles a variety of polls.

Science News (www.sciencenews.org).

Wayback Machine (archive.org): Internet archive that attempts to archive everything on the Internet, including pages that have disappeared from their original sites.

www.googleguide.com: A list of effective search methods, whether on a particular website or across the Internet.

NEWS VERIFICATION RESOURCES:

FactCheck (www.factcheck.org).

Politifact (www.politifact.com).

PunditFact (www.politifact.com/punditfact):
Truth and accuracy among opinion writers.

Snopes (www.snopes.com): Authoritative and
entertaining reports on all manner of stories, from
the serious to the amusing.

ACKNOWLEDGMENTS

I am grateful to my wife, Nancy Christy, who taught eighth-grade English in the Tulsa, Oklahoma, school system for seventeen years, for her support and suggestions. Thanks also to my agent, Alice Martell, and to my editor Lisa Westmoreland, publicists Daniel Wikey and Megan Perritt, creative director Emma Campion, production associate Heather Porter, and copy editor Kristi Hein.

ABOUT THE AUTHOR

Bruce Bartlett has worked in Washington for more than forty years in the House of Representatives, the U.S. Senate, the U.S. Treasury Department, and the White House. He has been chief of staff of a congressional committee and a syndicated columnist, and is the author of nine books, including two *New York Times* best sellers. He has been quoted innumerable times in major newspapers and appeared on countless radio and television programs. He and his wife, Nancy, live in Great Falls, Virginia.

INDEX